W9-CHN-365

ANDERSON ELEMENTARY SCHOOL LIBRARY

ANDERSON ELEMENTARY

What Do You See in a Cloud?

By Allan Fowler

Consultants

Robert L. Hillerich, Professor Emeritus,
Bowling Green State University, Bowling Green, Ohio;
Consultant, Pinellas County Schools, Florida

Lynne Kepler, Educational Consultant

Fay Robinson, Child Development Specialist

ANDERSON ELEMENTARY LIBRARY SCHOOL

ᑅ Children's Press®
A Division of Grolier Publishing
New York   London   Hong Kong   Sydney
Danbury, Connecticut

Project Editor: Downing Publishing Services
Designer: Herman Adler Design Group
Photo Researcher: Feldman & Associates, Inc.

Library of Congress Cataloging-in-Publication Data

Fowler, Allan.
    What do you see in a cloud? / by Allan Fowler.
      p. cm. – (Rookie read-about science)
    Includes index.
    Summary: Simple text and illustrations describe what clouds are
made of, how they differ, and why they fall back to earth as rain.
    ISBN 0-516-06056-2
    1. Clouds—Juvenile literature. [1. Clouds.] I. Title. II. Series.
QC921.35.F69   1996
551.57'6–dc20   95-39676
                                                 CIP
                                                 AC

Copyright 1996 by Children's Press®, Inc.
All rights reserved. Published simultaneously in Canada.
Printed in the United States of America.
1 2 3 4 5 6 7 8 9 10 R 05 04 03 02 01 00 99 98 97 96

You can see all kinds of
things when you look up
at clouds. One cloud could
be shaped like a fish . . .

another like a dog . . .

and another might remind
you of a spaceship.

What do you see
in *this* cloud?

Clouds often seem to be in
a hurry. The wind blows
them across the sky.

One moment you're touched
by the shadow of a cloud —

and a moment later you're
in bright sunshine.

Rain comes from clouds.

In fact, clouds are made
of water.

Every day a great amount
of water rises into the air
from oceans, rivers, lakes
— even from the leaves
of plants and trees.

11

It rises in the form of very tiny drops called water vapor.

You can't see water vapor, but it's all around you.

The water vapor cools off as it rises, or meets cold air, or passes over cold land or water.

When the water vapor has cooled enough, the droplets come together and make clouds.

Have you ever seen your
breath in front of your
face on a winter day?

Then you actually saw
a small cloud being
formed as your warm,
moist breath reached
the cold air.

ANDERSON ELEMENTARY SCHOOL LIBRARY

As the droplets in a cloud
get cooler, they run together
and make bigger drops —
big enough now to fall back
to earth as rain.

If the weather is cold
enough, the drops of water
freeze and fall as snow.

Clouds that are puffy like cotton are called cumulus clouds.

When cumulus clouds pile up like this, a thunderstorm may be coming.

Stratus clouds stretch across the sky in flat sheets.

Dark stratus clouds often
bring rain.

Cirrus clouds are thin,
wispy, and high in the sky.

Clouds that form just above the ground are called fog. Sometimes a fog is so thick, you can't see the other side of the street.

This is what it looks like when you fly in a plane above a layer of clouds.

You see the sun shining on the clouds. But people on the ground can't see the sun.

To them, it's just another cloudy day.

You might like
sunny days better
than cloudy ones.

But without clouds, there would be no rain.

Without rain, nothing
could grow — and
you'd have nothing
to eat.

So you can be glad
there are rain clouds —
as long as you don't
forget your umbrella.

Words You Know

rain

snow

cloud

cirrus cloud

cumulus cloud

stratus cloud

fog

31

Index

About the Author

Allan Fowler is a free-lance writer with a background in advertising. Born in New York, he lives in Chicago now and enjoys traveling.

Photo Credits

Valan Photos — ©Harold V. Green, cover; ©Ken Patterson, 8, 9; ©J.R. Page, 11
©John Elk III, 3
H. Armstrong Roberts — ©H. Abernathy, 4
Tom Stack & Associates — ©Bob Pool, 5; ©Thomas Kitchin, 17, 30 (top right)
Photo Edit — ©Rhoda Sidney, 6; ©David Young-Wolff, 15; ©Myrleen Ferguson, 26
Visuals Unlimited — ©Steve McCutcheon, 7; ©A.J. Copley, 21; ©Walt Anderson, 27, 30 (bottom)
Tony Stone Images, Inc. — ©Scott Dietrich, 12; ©Darryl Torckler, 20, 31 (bottom left); ©Steve Elmore, 25
Earth Scenes — ©Joe McDonald, 16; ©John Lemker, 22, 31 (top left)
Root Resources — ©Louise K. Broman, 18, 31 (top right)
David G. Houser — ©Jan Butchofsky-Houser, 19
SuperStock International, Inc. — ©D.C. Lowe, 23, 31 (bottom right)
Photri, Inc. — 29, 30 (top left)
COVER: Cumulus cloud

DATE DUE

#47-0108 Peel Off Pressure Sensitive

ANDERSON ELEMENTARY SCHOOL

105175214   551.576 FOW

What do you see in a cloud?